Just ask Je

FIFTY YEARS IN THE VILLAGE SHOP

Written by

Jenny Ward
and **Eric Ward** (1946-2006)
with additional material by
Jackie Taylor and David Ward

*Half of the profits from this book will be donated
to the Lincs & Notts Air Ambulance*

*Some names in this book have been changed to
avoid any unintended embarrassment.*

First published in Great Britain as
a softback original in 2022.

Copyright © Jenny Ward 2022.

All rights reserved.

ISBN 978-1-3999-3796-2

sacomms@icloud.com

When visitors to the village ask for directions, the response is usually...

'No idea... just ask Jenny at the shop!'

IN MEMORY OF MY HUSBAND ERIC

Contents

PART ONE
Eric's story p.9

PART TWO
Jenny's story p.43

PART THREE
David's story p.105

PART FOUR
Jackie's story p.119

I wish to thank...

All my loyal customers, many of whom have become good friends.

All my family for their help over the years; I couldn't have run the shop without them.

Digby and Ann for agreeing to edit, design and publish this book for us.

Jenny Ward
The Village Shop
Donington on Bain

Foreword

This story spans half a century of life in an open-all-hours village shop, run by a remarkable family, who have devoted almost every waking moment to hard work in the rural economy.

The shop nestles in the River Bain valley, in an *Area of Outstanding Natural Beauty,* and fifty years on, it continues to thrive, attracting loyal customers from miles around, including many grateful cyclists and walkers.

Near-universal car ownership and the remorseless ascendence of cut-throat urban supermarkets have seen the demise of countless village shops across the country. But not the Village Shop at Donington on Bain in the Lincolnshire Wolds.

Times have changed, of course. It no longer provides a mobile-shop service to surrounding villages, and its long trading hours have been slightly trimmed. But it's still open every day, except Christmas Day.

And whatever a customer wants, from paintbrush to Prosecco, coal to coffee (freshly-made)... well, Jenny has it all.

This is the gentle but spellbinding story of an extraordinary rural shopkeeping dynasty. *Enjoy!*—D.S.

PART ONE: ERIC'S STORY

From farming to shopkeeping

By Eric Ward

Fifty years ago, in 1973, my wife and I bought a rundown village shop in the middle of the Lincolnshire Wolds. Weekly takings were £150. Nothing had been spent on the property for some years.

The old sheds in the yard housed a stable, with hay-racks on the wall. There was a sand floor, and one broken door was hanging off its hinges.

Three weeks before we moved in, I spent several days going out with the previous owner on his daily round. I had to learn the round because that was going to be my part of the job. My wife in the shop, and me on the round. So we thought.

My wife's name is Jenny and we ran in her name. My name is Eric, my son is David and my daughter is Jackie. My son was three years old, my daughter, one. Jenny is five years my junior.

My wife already had shop experience, from before marrying me. I was a farmer and knew nothing of the business. My life was about to change completely.

By arrangement, I met the previous owner and got in his old damp and rattling car, and set off on the road on his rounds. It was January—dull, wet, cold and blustery. Being I was quite shy, I kept rather silent, but polite.

We pulled up outside the first house.

Announcing, 'This is my first call today', he got out, after struggling with the car door. He looked at me and said, 'Aren't you coming in with me?'

Reluctantly, I went in with him, down the garden path. In the back garden there were chicken pens with chickens paddling in four inches of squad.

On the right was a clothesline, a long clothesline full of dirty washing. There were nappies, nappies and more nappies on the line, and they all looked filthy. There were children's jumpers with holes in the sleeves, a boy's trousers, with half of one leg missing, a man's shirt and trousers, and underpants that needed seeing too. I think they were supposed to be white but they were very nearly black.

We turned a corner to the back of the house. Mr Richardson knocked on the back door, and walked in. I followed and the first thing to hit me was the smell. You know the smell—dirty washing, dirty people, dirty house. It stank to make your eyes run. It made you catch your breath. It was *awful.*

He shouted, 'We are here', and an alarmed voice sounded from the other room, 'It's the grocer kids. Get your bloody selves out of my way'.

She appeared from the front-room in a dirty worn-out dressing-gown, buttons all the way down the front, all undone. She was fat. She stank more than ever. She had big breasts, wobbling about under her so-called night dress.

'Hello. Sorry I'm not dressed, but I never am when you come Mr Richardson .'

The previous owner of the shop said, 'Let me introduce Mr Ward. He is taking over from me in three weeks and I am showing him the rounds.'

'Hello', she said to me. 'You don't look like a grocer to me, you look more like my old man. He works on the farm, for Smith's.'

'Hello', I said. 'Does he? You're right. I'm not a shopkeeper yet, but I hope I am soon.'

She started giving Mr Richardson her shopping list and he was writing it down. She suddenly said, 'Oh yes, and I want some more of that new washing powder you sold me last week. It's bloody grand! Have you seen how white my washing is this week?'

We thanked her for the order and left. When we got in his car, he looked at me and said, 'Well, what do you think to that one there?'

Then he laughed at me. Tears were running down my face from the stink in the house. It was in my throat, it was up my nose, it was on my clothes; it was terrible.

We did four calls that morning and after dinner, which I had with Mr Richardson and his wife at the shop, we did the four orders up in boxes and then went in his old car on the round to deliver them.

Eric and Jenny on their wedding day in 1969 at Walesby Church.

How much Mr Richardson took that day, I don't know. I was too shy, and cold, and wet, and fed-up, to take much notice of money on that first day.

I went with Mr Richardson once on each of his day's rounds. It was enough. He was rather offhand with the customers which I didn't take to very much. So I decided that once on each day of his round was enough to show me which houses to call on when I took over.

January 13 was the date we moved in. I was flitting myself with all our furniture on two four-wheel farm trailers, sheeted down with trailer-sheets. It's a good job the trailers were sheeted down, because that morning was just like my first time out on the rounds with Mr Richardson —wet and cold.

I arrived at the shop on my tractor with the first of the two trailer loads of furniture, with my wife eager to get into the shop.

My father and mother, and Jean Grant (a friend from a nearby village), and myself, were the staff and we were going to get busy scrubbing floors, laying carpets and lino and lifting in the furniture.

Mr and Mrs Richardson greeted me that morning and handed over the keys for the property. They wished us well, then got in their car, and left us to move in.

My wife, my mother and Jean set about cleaning the front-room first. It overlooked the road, so was the nearest to put the furniture in. The shop door was on the roadside as well, so my father and I could call my wife whenever a customer came shopping.

It really was very cold, so we decided we would light the old solid-fuel Esse cooker in the kitchen, to heat plenty of hot water for the ladies for scrubbing

Donington on Bain in the early 1900s: the village shop is the building immediately before the brewer's dray outside the Black Horse pub.

out with, and to get the house a bit warmer.

But we were in for a disappointment. The Esse refused to work. All it did was fill the kitchen with smoke.

By this time the three ladies were getting mad because they hadn't got any hot water for scrubbing-out. So we put on the immersion heater, and the kettle, and three saucepans of water on the electric cooker.

My father and I looked at, played with, discussed and examined the Esse but we couldn't get it to work. All it would do was fill the kitchen with smoke. So we decided to get on the phone and ring a firm that had the same year sold me an oil-fired catering range for the farmhouse where my parents still lived.

Yes, they would be pleased to sell me another Cleopatra oil-fired cooking range and deliver it next day.

The next problem was going to be getting a plumber at short notice to come next day to install the new cooker. But then I remembered that the plumber who installed the one at the farmhouse had said he was going to take a week off work in January, to catch up on odd jobs at home. So I found his number and gave him a call.

My luck was in. It was the very week he was having off from work and, yes, he would come the next day to oblige.

By this time it was just gone 10 o'clock in the morning and the three ladies had got the front-room cleaned out and were ready for my father and me to get the furniture in, out of the wet.

We decided it would be quickest to lift all the furniture in through the front-room window. Then we would leave it in the front-room until we got the other rooms scrubbed-out and decorated.

Eric with son David and daughter Jackie.

At this point my wife's parents arrived to collect David and Jackie. They were going to stay with them for three days, until we got the house sorted out.

At the end of that first day we were very tired and dirty. Except for one small fire in the living room, we hadn't got any heating in the place. And now it was starting to freeze.

The shop had been shut since 4.30pm and we had got our double-bed put up, but not made, and had got the children's bedrooms scrubbed out, ceilings emulsioned and the paintwork undercoated.

Jean had started papering the walls in what was going to be David's room.

My parents had left for home some time earlier and Jean had left at 7.30pm, promising she would see us next morning at about 9 o'clock.

Jenny and I sat down at the kitchen table and had a cup of coffee and we were both wondering if we had done the right thing... or had we bitten off more than we could chew?

Jenny said she was pleased her parents had taken our children home for a day or two because it wouldn't have been very nice for them until we got a bit straighter.

I reminded her that in the morning it was going to be my first round on my own.

Although there were only four calls to make, I had got to put the orders up in boxes, add them up, and deliver them, as well as collect the money. I would need a hand to put the orders up because I was not very sure what a lot of the things were called.

We went upstairs to make up our bed and have a wash, then go to bed, and leave everything as it was until morning.

It was very cold upstairs so we put two extra blankets on the bed to keep us warm.

It was the coldest night I have ever had in my life. It made no difference whether we cuddled up together or not; we were both freezing all night. The bed felt damp, and I suppose it could have been, seeing it had been moved from one house to another on such a wet day.

Morning arrived. We were up early having had a very bad night's sleep. It seemed so very different to be in this place, with no heating in the house or shop, and a keen frosty morning to greet us. I was feeling apprehensive, not knowing what the day was going to bring.

The shop seemed empty as I walked in from the house. It smelled odd, and it felt old. Everything I looked at seemed strange.

Jenny called through from the kitchen. 'Breakfast is ready and the bread van is here with the day's bread.'

I went outside with her to see the driver. It was still dark, and cold and frosty. I remember the driver saying, 'It talks of snow later. What bread do you want?'

Jenny said, 'We don't know. Can you tell us?'

How the village used to look: the Black Horse pub is on the left and the shop is next to it, with Eric's inconvenient narrow drive to the right of the shop.

The driver said it depended on what the other van had left in his box.

'Erm… what other van? What box are you on about?' I asked.

'Well,' he said, 'don't you know? I am Sunblest, but the other van, which comes about 4 o'clock, has Mother's Pride, and Richardsons always got off me what the other man didn't leave'.

This was great. We didn't know anything about another van. 'Richardson only told us about you coming. Where's the other box… do you know?'

'Well I think it's round the back, somewhere in the yard. That's where he went when I was early one day.'

So we all went round to seek the box. 'It's there in the corner, I think,' said the driver.

We located it. It was made of plywood and appeared to have been there for years. Inside were four Mother's Pride large white-sliced loaves, a ticket for the bread, and a note which read, 'You forgot to leave a list of what you wanted so have left the same as yesterday'.

'Well, what do you want off me now you've found it?' asked the driver. All we could tell him was, 'Can you leave the same as yesterday? We will see how we go, because we don't really know what we need.'

'Okay, that will be just three large white-sliced breads then.'

'Okay, if you say so—that will do.'

We went back into the kitchen and had our breakfast. I always have a full fried breakfast every day, except on Sundays. I think this is something to do with being born and bred on a farm.

You always had to have a good breakfast when I was a boy. It set you up for a day out in the fields in all sorts of weather, and I'm sure it's why the weather never seemed to bother me.

If it's wet or cold, frosty or snowy, if you get a good

breakfast and you keep busy, you don't feel the cold. But once you stop working you very soon feel miserable if you are wet. But if you keep busy you generate your own heat as you work.

We finished breakfast and I put on my jacket and my trilby hat. I've always worn a trilby hat, ever since I was 21 years old.

Jenny watched me getting ready to go on my first day's round on my own. She asked me if I'd got my notebook, and had I got a pen? Did I know where I was going? If someone asked for something I didn't know anything about, she said I must write it down and she would sort it out when I got back to the shop.

Dilapidated old street-facing buildings in the yard were pulled down; they made reversing onto the road hazardous.

'Okay, Jenny,' I said. 'I'm off. Bye.'

I got in my car and backed out of the entrance into the road, and it was at this point that I decided the first thing I must get done was to knock down the old buildings on the roadside, because my access to the back of the shop was very narrow and the house and shop, and all the old buildings, were straight on the roadside.

So when you backed out of the yard you couldn't see whether anything was coming, and though it's a quiet road, sooner or later I was going to drive out in front of another vehicle and have a smash.

All the old buildings were no good anyway. There was a barn next to our house, after the drive, which was only a sad drive anyway. The barn had a granary in the top. I assume this is where they kept all the hay and best oats for the horses.

Years ago it was joined on to an old falling-down house which I understand was for the man who looked after the horses to live in.

This had a large washhouse at the back where, when you stood on what was supposed to be the lawn, you could touch the roof. This gives you a guide as to how high the ground was behind all the buildings.

By now I had got to my first call and as I got out of my car I wondered if she would smell as much as she did the first day, with Mr Richardson.

The clothesline was still there, but it was empty. I knocked on the door and waited for a reply. I thought it might look bad if I walked straight in, but Mr Richardson had.

A woman's voice shouted out. 'Come in. Don't stand out there knocking all day.' So I took a deep breath of fresh air, remembering what it was like last time I came, and walked in. I blinked and caught my breath; it was *worse* than last time.

'Hello' she said.

'Morning Mrs Beecham.'

'Don't you start by calling me Mrs Beecham. I only use first names. What are we going to call you?'

'Eric is my Christian name.'

'My name is Lesley. Call me Lesley. Now don't mind the kids, especially the baby, he always runs around with no clothes on till dinner time when his Dad comes in.

'I didn't want him but he came just like the other-ones. His Dad is such a randy sod you know.

'Now where have I put that book? I have decided I

will have a different system with you. That other chap would never leave me a bill, so I've got this book. You can take it back with you, then I will have a bill when you come back, won't I?

'You want to get a van you know. He used to have a van but it fell to bits and he said it wasn't worth getting another one.'

All five of her children were standing around me, quiet as a mouse, just watching; all dressed in rough, dirty clothes, except for the little one, who didn't have a stitch on.

The air in the house was really getting to me by now and I could feel my eyes starting to run.

'Are you alright?' she asked. 'You look as if you're crying.'

'Yes, I'm fine thank you. It must be the cold I've got.' On opening her order book I started to read the list…

10lb sugar
7 bottles milk
½lb tea
1lb lard
2oz tobacco

> 6 boxes matches
>
> 1 packet of candles
>
> 1 ST
>
> 1 jam
>
> 1 cigarette papers.

I looked up at her, and she said, 'Is that okay?'

She wrote 'Saturday' down underneath, and added, 'You can add it all up for me to pay you when you come.'

'That's fine,' I said. 'See you later.' I opened the door and felt the fresh air come rushing in.

'How long before you are back?' she asked.

'Just after dinner I think, if that's alright.'

'Come any time. I'm not going anywhere. Bye.'

I went out, pulled the door shut behind me, hurried down the garden path, jumped in my car, and started to cough. I could taste the house in my mouth. It was really horrible. I couldn't get rid of it. My eyes were stinging, tears running down my cheeks. I started the car, wound the windows down for fresh air, and drove off.

My next call was as different again. One old lady on her own in a fairly new bungalow. A nice old lady… I was going to get on with this one, I thought.

She had a small pet dog which was very friendly with me last time I was here. I knocked on the door and a moment or two later she opened the door.

'Hello, you're early aren't you? Come on in and have a sit down. The kettle's just on the boil. Do you want sugar in your tea?'

'Well, yes please,' I replied, more in surprise than anything.

'Don't stand in the hall. Come in the kitchen and talk to me. Mr Richardson used to tell me all the gossip, you know, so you will have to do that job now, won't you?

'Do you take milk? Come in the kitchen and talk to me. I don't spend much time in the other rooms now that I'm on my own. I just live in here. I've got my dog and my radio, but I like callers. You know, something to look forward to.

'There you are, do you want a biscuit with your tea?

'Mr Richardson used to stay at least an hour with me, telling me everything that goes on in the village. You'll do the same, won't you?'

I was thinking like mad what to say in reply. I

heard myself saying, 'I'm sorry, but I can't. I've got to get back to the shop because the plumber is supposed to be coming today to put the new cooker in the kitchen and he can't lift it on his own.'

She said. 'Haven't you got any heating in your place then? It must be very cold like that.'

'It is,' I said, 'so I must go. Can I have your order please? The plumber must be there by now.'

'Well, I've got a new book… but you don't look as if you would diddle an old lady. The last thing on my list is best beef. It's got to be the best. I only have the best joints, alright?'

I gulped down my tea and biscuit and thanked her for her order.

My next two customers were out but they had both left a list on the door, so I was on my way back to the shop with four orders, feeling fairly pleased with the way I had got away from the nice old lady.

I had a feeling that when Mr Richardson was out on his rounds he did a lot more talking than selling. That wouldn't do for me. I'd got to get on and get some goods sold, not spend time gossiping with customers.

I arrived back at the shop and the first person I saw was Jean. She was filling her bucket with clean water at the kitchen sink. She was busy cleaning the bathroom upstairs.

I went into the shop and found Jenny so we could make the orders up for me to deliver in the afternoon.

She was standing behind the new till we had bought, trying to get used to it by practising with all the buttons to see if she could add up alright with it.

It wasn't a very expensive till. More an adding machine on a cash drawer, and it was operated by handle, not by electric. But it was better than the box Mr Richardson had used.

As we started doing the orders, Jenny said to me, 'What size 'ST' does she want?'

'What size?' I replied. 'How am I supposed to know that, when I don't even know what an 'ST' is?'

She burst out laughing.

'What's so funny, Jenny?'

'Don't you really know what 'ST' stands for?'

'No I don't and I didn't ask the customer either, as I didn't want to show my ignorance. I just assumed you would know.'

'It stands for sanitary towels,' she explained, still laughing. Well how was I supposed to know that?

'And what washing powder does she want?'

'I don't know that either, only that it was supposed to be a new one that Mr Richardson sold her some weeks ago, and she said it was a lot better than the old powder that she used before.'

So we chose Ariel, as that was reputed to be a good one.

It took quite a long time to do those four orders. Everything I did seemed very new to me. The smell of the shop and the smell of all the goods I handled doing the order, and the sound of all the fridges and freezers running in the background.

One fridge would be running, then another would start up, then another. Then the first one would stop, just as if they were in competition with one another. And the noise the till made when Jenny used it.

And it was at that moment that it hit me... all the goods the customers wanted, that we didn't have on the shelves. Just about half our shop was empty and it should have been full.

I decided then that we would have to do a large order from our Mace grocery suppliers, and it was going to be a difficult job, because what should we buy? We didn't know what the customers were going to want.

The shop always sold an excellent Fonseca port, because it was Eric's favourite tipple; note the glass on the window-sill.

And at least a quarter of the goods in the shop looked as if they had been there for some time. The shelves were dirty and hadn't been painted for years. Come to that, none of the shop had been painted for years.

At that point the shop door opened and in walked a lorry driver. 'Can you help me? I'm looking for Mr

Ward in Donington on Bain and someone told me this was Donington-on-Bain, but they'd lived in the village for 30 years and didn't know where Mr Ward lived.'

'Yes,' I said. 'You've found him. What have you bought… a cooker or a diesel tank?'

'A cooker. It's heavy. Have you got something to lift it off with?'

'Sorry, only two of us here, three with you. But we might be able to get it off the side of the lorry if you back it into the yard and we can get it on the grass bank.'

'Let's have a look,' he said. So I took him in the yard and told him what I was talking about.

'Hell, this doesn't look very handy, does it?'

'Well if you back it in and I get some planks we should have a better idea if it's going to work,' I said.

He was not convinced, but replied, 'Well, will you watch me in? I don't want to bend my lorry.'

He got backed in okay. He obviously knew his wagon pretty well. He got right up to the grass bank and we laid planks from the bank onto the lorry, then slid the cooker onto the bank.

The driver was happy. He got his ticket and left.

Jenny was busy putting the four orders out of the way in the storeroom, so she didn't stumble over them whilst serving customers in the shop.

I asked her, 'Are we going to have any dinner today?' Until now I hadn't thought about dinner, but I supposed we would have something.

'I'll see what they want upstairs,' said Jenny. 'Shall I go, or will you ask them?'

'I'll ask them.' So upstairs I went and I couldn't help noticing the different smell. As I got on the landing there was a nice smell of disinfectant and new paint. It was much more of a homely smell than when we went to bed the night before.

I found my mother and Jean in what was going to be our bedroom. They had just finished scrubbing it out. I asked Mother, 'How are you getting on? The place is beginning to smell better.'

'By God, that's your father for you; that's just the sort of thing your father would say.'

'Where is Father today? Is he okay?'

'Yes, he's alright. He said he wouldn't be here until dinner because he had to sort some of the pigs this morning and the delivery lorry with the pig-meal was coming.'

'Well, it's dinner time now and I came to see what you want.'

'Oh, just a sandwich and a cup of tea will do for us. We'll come down for it. Don't you think we've got on well today? We've got all the rooms up here except the bathroom scrubbed out, so we'll get David's room papered after dinner, and probably start on Jackie's room as well. Don't you think Jean?'

'Yes, I finished scrubbing the bathroom out yesterday before I went home, but we'll have to do them again once we get them papered.'

'Yes', said Mother, 'and we'll be able to make a better job next time because we'll have plenty of hot water once the plumber gets the new cooker working.'

We went down to the kitchen and Jenny made sandwiches for us all.

'Oh, they look good Jenny,' said Mother. 'Don't do many for me. I only want two or three and Father won't want many; he's not very keen on sandwiches. I'll make tea, shall I? How many cups do we want?'

'Just mugs Mother, not cups. You don't mind a mug do you Jean?'

'No, I don't mind. We use mugs at home anyway. Now, have you got a bit of meat on the go? Your father much prefers it to sandwiches.'

Just then, my father walked in, and said, 'I see your cooker has come. What a funny place to put it.'

'That's the only place I could think of that was near enough to get it off the lorry. It's really, really heavy,' I said.

Father said, 'The lorry driver came to me at the farm first. He thought it a bit odd, as he'd brought the other one only recently. I had to direct him to here so I knew you'd got your cooker.

'The plumber can't come until tonight. He rang me at the farm because he hadn't got this phone number.'

'Bloody hell', I thought, 'We were getting on well—so there had to be something to go wrong.'

I looked at Father. 'What are you doing this afternoon?'

He promised, 'I'll keep the ladies hard at it and sort out any problems that come up until you get back, then I'll help you get this old cooker out ready for the plumber coming tonight.'

'Thanks,' I said, swilling my last drop of tea. 'I'll get the orders delivered now and see you later.' I loaded the orders into the car and left for my first call. You can probably guess where….

As I knocked on the door with the order in my arms, I braced myself, ready to be hit with that ghastly smell. 'Come in,' shouted the customer. Taking a deep breath, I went in.

'Put it on the sink and I'll be there in a minute.'

Putting the order down on the draining board, I looked around the room. It was cluttered with everything you could think of.

There was an old-fashioned cooking range, with a back boiler. The door to the top oven was open and over it hung a row of children's underpants.

The fire was drawing properly, and there was a kettle, a very black kettle, set on the pan holder, which was half on and half off the fire. It was boiling its head off. Bits of burnt wood were dropping off the fire onto the large hearth which these old cooking ranges had.

The main oven door was just open and there was something cooking, but I couldn't see what it was. To the right was a large pile of wood, ready for burning.

Half-way up the wall was a shelf full of packets of groceries, which looked as if the smoke from the fire had discoloured them. To the left of the fire was a heap of something that looked like rags. The floor was bare red stone, brick-size, put in diagonal rows

As Eric's delivery round increased in popularity, a bigger, walk-in, vehicle was required. She was called 'Elizabeth'.

across the floor from corner to corner.

There was a metal-legged, three-by-three foot table. Next to this, another heap of rags covered in what must have had at least an inch of household dirt, which presumably had built up over a very long time.

On the top of the table were dirty nappies waiting to be washed, and at the side of them, on the same table, was a tea cup, an open bag of sugar, and a bottle of milk.

Next was a kitchen cabinet. It had no doors left on it and only one drawer, which was half open. It had some cutlery in it. Next along the wall was a brush and dusters, which looked as if they hadn't been used

The village came out to watch as Eric walked daughter Jackie to the Church on her wedding day.

for weeks.

The ceiling was a very dark brown colour, just like smoked bacon. The back of the door was loaded with coats of all sizes and colours.

The stairs door had been ripped off its hinges so you could see the stairs, which had nothing on them, except dirt.

By now my eyes were beginning to run from the strength and density of the odour. The conclusion

I reached was that nothing in this house had been washed down, cleaned out or disinfected for years!

It was definitely the worst place I had seen in my life. I didn't think people really lived like this. It was a bloody scandal, really.

You can imagine all the germs and bugs. They would have floored most people—but they left this family alone. Mum, Dad, and five small children all under school age, seemed quite healthy and didn't suffer from anything, except maybe a bit of cold.

- *This is where Eric Ward's notes end abruptly. He always intended to continue the story, but life at the village shop became too hectic, as he and Jenny set about growing turnover, then added a timber business, based a few hundred yards away. Deciphering his notes has been a challenge; daughter Jackie Ward, now Jackie Taylor, typed up his woodyard orders for him as she grew older, and she recalls the vanishingly small chances of carrying out the task with any reasonable expectation of accuracy.*

Plenty
Post Cards
Murray Mints
BOUNTY
TWIX
TWIX
Semolina
HOVIS

HOT DRINKS
AVAILABLE
IN SHOP

I SHALL CLOSE
From 10 am Monday 19th Sep
FOR THE QUEEN'S
Funeral
so Please come early FOR your
Papers
Thank you oo

£1.19

£1

6	6	6	6
OF THE BEST	OF THE BEST	OF THE BEST	OF THE BEST

Cadbury

PART TWO: JENNY'S STORY

Anything to keep our customers happy

By Jenny Ward

I run the only traditional village shop in the Lincolnshire Wolds that's still open all hours, every day except Christmas Day.

Yet 50 years ago, when my husband Eric and I bought the shop, it was almost on a whim. We just happened to be passing and saw the 'For Sale' sign.

Being a shop-keeper, you get to know your customers and their families… the joy of children being born, the sadness of death, the successes, worries, trials and tribulations.

I have watched my customers' children grow up and get jobs, leave the village, get married, and come back to the village with their children to see Granny and Grandad.

When you watch people from behind the counter, you see family traits passing down the line.

During my time as a shop-keeper I have seen almost all the other village shops in the area close. Benniworth, Hemingby, Scamblesby, Burgh on Bain, Ludford, Market Stainton, Goulceby and Hainton are all within a ten-mile radius, and all have lost their shop.

Fortunately the Post Offices at East Barkwith and Donington on Bain continue to thrive. But you have to go some way to find other rural Post Offices.

My maiden name was England and I come from the village of Walesby, which is about eight miles from our Donington on Bain shop.

I married Eric Ward 54 years ago, in June 1969, and we lived nearby at Poplar Farm, Goulceby, where Eric farmed. Eric died from cancer on November 12, 2006. It was my personal tragedy. I still miss him so

Eric died from cancer on November 12, 2006. It was my personal tragedy. I still miss him so much. We all do.

much. We all do.

We have a son and a daughter, David and Jackie. Jackie married Matthew Taylor in July 1993. On her wedding day, Eric walked her through the village to the church at Donington on Bain and the street was lined with villagers.

They have two sons—Jake, who was born in May 2000, and Luke, born October 2001.

Our son David married Sally at East Barkwith in July 1997. They have three children—Katie, born April 1998, Rebecca, born March 2001, and James, born May 2003.

So how did we come to be a family of Lincolnshire Wolds shop-keepers?

We had sold the farm at Goulceby and didn't really know what we wanted to do. Initially we thought we might grow vegetables at Sotby, a small village about four miles away.

But then in November 1972 we were driving two friends home through Donington on Bain and saw the village shop for sale. Leaving our friends Eileen and David in the car with our children, we got out to have a look round. A few weeks later we bought the shop, and we moved in on January 13, 1973.

Our son, David, was two years old, and daughter Jackie, 11 months.

She was in her pram in the shop window on a cold frosty morning when my parents, Phylis and Reg England, came in their little green minivan to collect her and David to stay at Walesby Grange for a week.

I needed to concentrate on the shop. We had only £150 worth of stock, so orders had to be made to fill the shelves. Meanwhile Eric would be concentrating on the small van round, which had to be built up.

Our friend Jean Grant came to clean and decorate

When we bought the shop, it had only £150 worth of goods. These days we aim to stock everything our customers are likely to need, including basics ranging from paintbrushes to yeast.

the four bedrooms. Eric's Mum, Barbara, also helped. His Dad, Claude, fetched furniture from our old home at Goulceby, with a tractor and trailer, putting it in the house through the front-room window.

The buildings outside needed to be emptied and knocked down, because they were dangerous.

Those early days are still vivid in my memory. There's a house near Benniworth Haven called 'Wayside Cottage'—it's still there today—and when we first came to the shop the Boy Scouts used it as a base for their summer camp.

On their last day, they could come in pairs into the shop to spend their money on sweets. They didn't have very much, but lots of the sweets then were four for 1p—Black Jacks, Fruit Salad and others.

Nowadays they cost anything up to 10p each, or two shillings in old money. When decimalisation came in we had to change all the prices in the shop.

In summer the shop window would be full of wasps. The waste land across the road, which is now 'Green Acres', always had wasp nests on it. Eric would watch where the wasps were going, then go and deal with them. The village children used to play there, so it needed to be clear of wasps if possible.

Jackie and Matthew built their house on the site of an old milking parlour, cleaning and using the original bricks.

We've seen many changes in the village over the years. Ben Truman had milking cows and would fetch them twice a day and walk them down the road to Old School Lane to his milking parlour. That milking parlour is now the home of my daughter Jackie and her husband Matthew, and they run it as a successful bed-and-breakfast.

Originally it was a Wesleyan Chapel, then a school, then a milking parlour. Jackie and Matthew knocked it down, cleaned every brick, and built their house, which they have called 'The Old School'.

Over the years we had three delivery vans. First a small grey van, then a green one, and finally a larger walk-in mobile shop we called *Elizabeth*. From this we would sell groceries on our regular rounds. And as it had a freezer in it, we could also sell ice-cream and frozen food.

We took this van all over the place—gymkhanas at the nearby Stenigot Estate, the 'Wheels' event at Manby airfield, the Hay Days at The Beeches, which were held for the Vera Dean cancer charity, cricket matches at Stenigot and bonfire nights at Henry Smith's farm at Withcall.

Soon after we had arrived at the shop we started building up the van round. When customers telephoned orders through for Eric, he would deliver them in the van, so if they had missed anything off their lists, they could get it on the van.

Meanwhile more things were being sold in the shop, which meant more places had to be found to keep stock on the shelves.

Cash-and-carry used to deliver once a week (and still do) and Eric would go to the Macdonald's factory in Louth once a week to collect hot pork pies and pastries. He would then call at customers on the way home, to deliver orders.

One day he stopped at Kimpsons, at Welton-le-

Wold, which is about five miles away. They used to take stray dogs in from the police. And this particular day they had a little golden Labrador puppy. Eric bought him for £5 and it came home with him in the van. By the time he reached the shop, the puppy had eaten 1lb of sausages! We called him 'Port'.

As the shop is in the centre of the village we see everything that's going on. For instance in summer 1973, whilst arranging various goods outside, I heard a tremendous noise, children shouting and screaming. Looking down the street, I saw lots of buses outside the village school. Of course! It was the junior schools intersports day.

Over the years we've had many different suppliers, with some firms closing or changing their delivery areas, and others taking their place.

Fruit and vegetables were supplied by Stevensons, of Louth, then from Shaws, of Fulstow.

Sterilised milk in tall bottles (now called Clover milk), with a halfpenny for returned bottles, was delivered from the nearby village of Market Stainton, then later by Brian Bates, of Market Rasen. These days it comes from our wholesaler.

Initially fresh bread was delivered by both Sunblest and Mother's Pride. Lyons cakes were also delivered once a week.

More recently we got our bread from Curtis of Lincoln, and now it comes from Starbucks, of Market Rasen, and from our wholesaler.

We still sell Dennetts ice-cream, made in Spilsby (only 15 miles away), as well, of course, as the usual Walls varieties.

When we first came here we sold Bellamy's pop and if you returned the empty bottle, you got some money back. The children in the village would go looking for the bottles, so they could bring them in, get the money, and spend it on sweets.

Our customers' buying habits have changed over the years. For instance, we arranged a Calor Gas agency, having undertaken to keep the containers in a locked compound. And we sold lots, as there was no mains gas in the village. We also sold a lot of paraffin for lighting and heating. But now, none at all.

Newspapers and magazines came from W.H. Smith. For many years they were left, at 5am, in the shop doorway. If I heard it raining on the bedroom window I had to get up quickly to bring them in, so they didn't get wet.

One day some boys from the village pinched the returns (these are any unsold papers from the day before) and littered them all the way to Louth.

It was after this that we had security cameras fitted, covering both up and down the road. Generally, as you might imagine, we are a very low-crime area, but the police did make use of the cameras when nearby sheds and property were burgled.

It took them about four hours to take the recordings they wanted, during which time I fed them tea and sandwiches (no charge).

Papers were left in the doorway at 5am. If it rained I had to get up quickly and bring them in, before they got wet.

We had a large blue metal bin made to keep the papers dry. It's still in use today. People often use it as a seat, whilst they drink their coffee, or eat their ice-cream.

In the 1980s we started selling Sunday papers. We took these over from the Stubbs family. We also did Green Shield Stamps. Customers saved up books and exchanged them for goods from what is now Argos.

On Mondays, the van round was quite small, only covering Asterby and Goulceby. Tuesday was North Withcall, Biscathorpe, Burgh on Bain, Girsby, Hainton, East Barkwith and South Willingham.

An old blind couple lived in South Willingham and when Eric called on them he would always wind up the clock for them. He would also write their Christmas cards. Next call was Benniworth, and then it was back to the shop to stock up for the next day.

On Wednesdays, the van stayed at home. This was the day we would have it serviced if necessary, and Eric would always be at home in the morning, so I could go into town.

On Thursdays he went to Withcall, Goulceby, Stenigot, Ranby, Sotby, Hainton, and then home.

Fridays were Biscathorpe, Burgh on Bain, Hain-

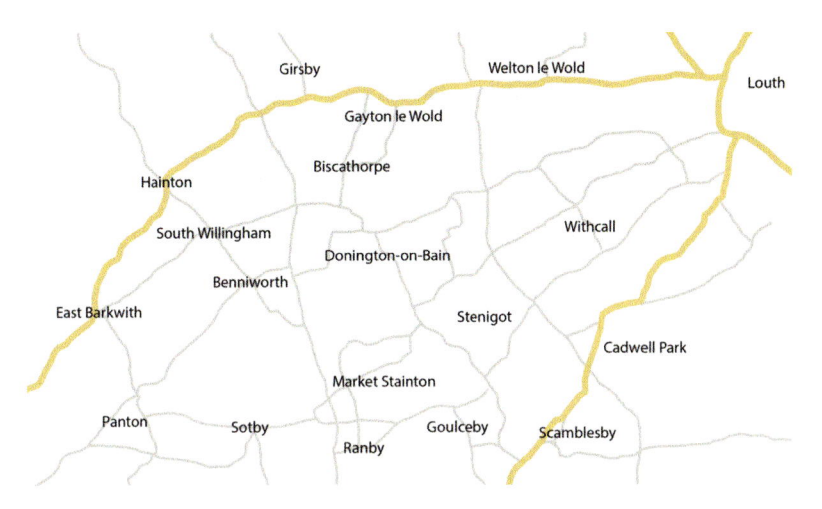

Our mobile shop was out and about five days a week, serving customers across much of the Lincolnshire Wolds.

ton, South Willingham and Benniworth and then on to Cadwell, where the house he called at was at the side of the race-track, so the van did some of the circuit. Next stop was Belchford, and then home.

On Saturday mornings he would deliver some orders in the village and then to North Withcall. He would come back down Welsdale Road to deliver the rest of the orders.

Some days the round was done very quickly. This was when Eric noticed pigeons in the fields. He would take his gun and get the pigeons off the farmers' crops. One day he managed to shoot over 200 birds.

July would find me picking strawberries in the

I am pictured here outside the shop, in 2011, with my good friends Eileen Peach (left) and Annie Cullen (right).

evenings—1,000lbs each summer—to sell in the shop. While I was picking, Eric would serve in the shop. He didn't know where everything was, or the prices, and he got a little flummoxed and flustered. He knew his van inside out, but not the shop.

He used to leave me notes saying so and so hadn't paid 'because I didn't know the price.' Fortunately our customers were trustworthy.

One night a customer came in and asked Eric for a packet of white sauce mix. 'Not got time to make my own,' he explained.

Next day, after eating the lunch he had so carefully prepared, his wife stared balefully at the sauce on her plate and exclaimed, 'From a packet!'

These customers were Paul and Annie Cullen. They went to France but Annie's almost 100-year-old Mother was still here, and for four years Annie travelled back and stayed with me for two nights when she went to see her Mum. In 2018 they moved back to England, down south. I don't see her now and I miss her.

When we first came to the shop, we would close on Christmas Day, Boxing Day and New Year's Day. But now papers are printed everyday except Christmas Day, so that's the only day we're shut. Even so, you can sure a customer will come knocking at the back door in a panic, having forgotten something!

The shop opened long hours, 6.30am to 8.30pm, Monday to Saturday, and 6.30am to 5pm on Sundays. We did this to keep customers happy and satisfied. This has always been our way.

We made very rare exceptions from time to time. For instance, the village football club used to sponsor a 12-mile walk on a Sunday morning. When this happened, we put off opening the shop until noon, so the whole family could do the walk together.

Another time was in 2022, on the bank holiday marking the funeral of Her Majesty the Queen. I did open the shop, but only until 10am, as I wanted to watch the whole ceremony myself.

The children were small when we moved to the shop. We had a board door between the internal shop door and the house so I could keep an eye on them and they could see me.

Two years after we arrived, Lynne Parkinson, and her sister-in-law Rosemary Parkinson, started a playgroup which David and Jackie attended before they started school.

As they grew older, they had to help in the shop, and go on the van rounds. Although the youngest, Jackie was the keenest to serve in the shop at teatime.

At the time, and just among ourselves, we referred to one customer as 'Dew Drop'.

I still blush when I recall how he came into the shop one day when Jackie was serving. He would have wanted cigarettes and at that time there was no legal restriction preventing her selling them.

'Yes, Dew Drop, what can I do for you?' said Jackie, as we listened in horror from the adjoining room.

Well how was she to know 'Dew Drop' was a pet name, only for use by us, in private?

Five years after we came to the shop, we got a licence to sell alcohol—another string to our bow. We also had videos of popular films to rent. These were superseded by DVDs and Blue-ray. But their day has been and gone, so we don't do them now.

In due course, David left school and went to run the East Barkwith shop and Post Office five miles away, which we bought in 1976.

Mike Chambers, a school friend of David's, used to buy his paper there every morning on his way to work. One morning he opened his paper and found a £50 note inside. How it got there remains a mystery.

In due course our green van became too small for all the goods Eric needed to carry on his rounds, so we bought a much larger red mobile shop. We called her *Elizabeth*. Eventually Jackie started to take her out on the rounds, allowing Eric to give more time to his wood business, felling trees on the Wallis, Girsby, Oxcombe, Wykeham and Stenigot estates.

He would fell the trees in early spring, just as the sap was rising. It was usually very cold and the wood felt like icicles in the back of the trucks.

We used to sell logs and sticks from Eric's woodyard. He would bring home all the 'slipeings' (the sawn-off outer edges of large tree trunks) and saw them up, then I would chop them into kindling sticks and bag them up and sell them in the shop.

One day I heard the saw stop and was worried he might have cut himself. He had. He'd cut the end of his thumb off. Jackie had to take him to Louth Hospital. The pain was so bad they had to stop on the way at Parkinson's farm and get some baler band to tie it up.

They wouldn't look at it at Louth and sent him to Lincoln by ambulance.

Jackie (by now a young Mum) had to come home as she was still breast feeding. I said I would go to the East Barkwith shop and wait for the ambulance to go past. It didn't—they had sent him in a car. He was still in the waiting room when I got there. He was in all his work clothes, and in lots of pain.

They said he would have to stay in overnight and the doctor saw him on the Saturday morning. He came home on the Sunday but the thumb had to be dressed each day. Jackie was his nurse. The end of his thumb was still on the saw bench when he came home. He had to rest for a short while but was soon back at the woodyard, where he soon managed to cut his finger—and once again Jackie had to be nurse and dress it.

At the shop, we sold logs by the trailer-load and by the bag. Between serving customers, I chopped sticks into bags to sell as kindling. I also made home-made fruit-loaves, as customers had no time to bake for themselves during the potato and sprout harvests. The sprout factory was at Stenigot.

I still make and sell cakes to order.

I needed a bigger kitchen for my baking. So one Monday morning I decided to knock the small pantry out, to provide more space.

When Eric came home from the van round, all the wood and shelving was outside. What a mess! He had to plaster part of the kitchen ceiling, and you can still see today where it was done.

After a year or so at the shop, we decided to hold a Christmas Show, buying in toys, chocolates, books and presents.

We used our front-room for this, for a week in October. Customers could come and choose things to put away in our Christmas Club for Santa to collect.

One year we had a visit from Father Christmas.

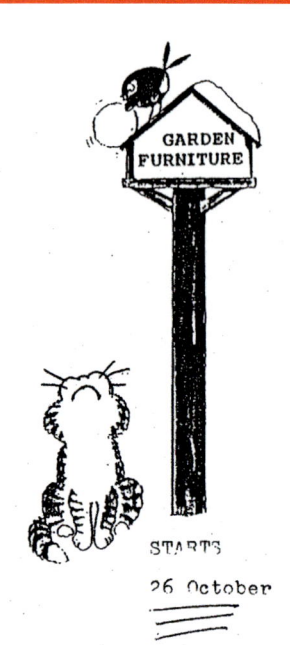

The Mace Store
Donington on Bain
Telephone: STENIGOT 287

Jenny and Eric

INVITE YOU, YOUR FAMILY AND FRIENDS

TO OUR

CHRISTMAS SHOW

FOR 8 DAYS ONLY

ALL DAY

STARTS
26 October

9 o clock am to 10 o clock pm

FINISHES
2 November

EACH DAY

We Have an Extensive Range of:-
**GARDEN FURNITURE - TOYS - BOOKS - JIGSAWS - SILVER AND BRASS - CHOCOLATES AND CONFECTIONERY
GIFTS FOR LADIES AND GENTLEMEN**
Which will be on display in our Snooker room - Call in Anytime of the Day or Evening and look around at your leisure.
You can make instant purchases or we will reserve any of the goods for you if you are in our CHRISTMAS CLUB.

There's Something for Everyone

WE WILL BE PLEASED TO SEE YOU

Orders Taken Now for:-
Christmas Trees, Christmas Cakes and Christmas Poultry

Strangely, we never saw Santa and Eric's Uncle Frank in the room at the same time!

The show was so successful we decided to do it every year. It soon outgrew our front room, so we used Eric's snooker shed instead. No snooker in the evenings for a week, for him and his pals.

Ever since 2007 I have put a big Father Christmas in our front-room window, which faces the street. He moves his arms and head about and the children can see him on their way to school. He comes out at the beginning of December and disappears on Christmas Eve (so he can go and deliver presents).

Eric's wood business always came into its own during the winter. As well as felling timber on local estates, he used to cut wood for Phil Dukes at a pallets firm in Lincoln. We had two Land-Rovers to deliver the logs to customers, to keep them going through the cold months.

In really bad snow, the roads would be blocked but Eric would go across the fields and hedge tops to meet the bread van at Louth, to get bread for the shop. As I've already mentioned, he did a lot of pigeon shooting and he knew his way around the fields as well as the roads. Keeping our customers happy has always been our aim.

If we were unable to get out with the van, orders were taken round in a Land-Rover both day and night.

Changes have continued apace over the years. For instance, when the National Lottery started, our East Barkwith shop was one of the first to get a machine to sell tickets. Louth didn't have any machines, so other than us, Grimsby (18 miles away) was the nearest place to buy them.

Consequently, David was very busy. I would collect people's tickets in my shop and then Eric would take them to East Barkwith on a Thursday.

I sell anything! If it's not in the shop it may well be in the kitchen, or I can get it in a few days. Customers have often exclaimed, 'Jenny, you could sell snow to an Eskimo!'

I enjoy sharing ideas for meals and giving advice on how to make things, and how to help older people. Everyone says, 'Just ask Jenny.'

In the past I've sold babies' bottles to feed cade lambs and fishing nets to clean out garden ponds or catch crayfish at Biscathorpe. My cakes went all over the country with customers visiting relatives.

During a sugar shortage we bought sugar in hundredweight sacks and rationed it out. We weighed it out and put it into blue bags for sale. We found these bags in the sheds when we took over the shop. Fortunately we had kept them—and they came in very useful.

In deep mid-winter, customers walked to the shop and we would give them a cup of tea to warm them up, and during a power failure we even finished off baking cakes and bread for customers, as Jackie was telling people, 'Take it to the shop; the oil-fired oven is always on.' We took many cups of tea and soup to the old people across the road.

When visitors to the village ask for directions, the response is often, 'No idea… just ask Jenny at the shop'.

People have come into the shop, left their dog tied-up outside, and then gone home without it. Anybody who has lost a pet will be told, 'Tell Jenny. She'll spread the word among her customers.'

There have been times when disruption to the day-to-day running of the shop has been unavoidable.

One of the biggest jobs we did was to renew the shop floor. This was done on a Tuesday afternoon and Wednesday morning. We had to shut the shop, but the van was in, so customers could use it to do their shopping.

In the shop, the middle aisle of goods was removed and the old wooden floorboards were taken up and chopped into sticks. Ballast was used to fill in a foot-deep hole, and early on the Wednesday morning a ready-mix concrete wagon arrived. We levelled it off as best we could, with just a slight slope to the counter to give it character. Customers complained the shop wasn't the same as it was too quiet: the floor didn't creak. But they soon got used to it.

On a bank holiday weekend in 1990 we were asked to do a van round selling milk, bread, papers and anything else our customers wanted at the Wheels motorsport event at Manby.

One customer, Ken Slavin, of Hainton (who used to renovate Land-Rovers and export them to the third-world countries), took a photo of *Elizabeth*. He had it framed and presented it to us as a present. It still hangs in the hall today.

Rooftop hooliganism: Eric puts a pram on newly-weds' roof, just before they were due to return from honeymoon.

In 2000, the van rounds stopped, as Jackie, who had taken them over from Eric, was pregnant with her first son. In any case, older people had passed on and the people who were buying their houses were out at work during the week, so quite often there was no-one at home to deliver to.

It was the end of an era for us and for our customers in the surrounding villages; it was also an indication of the way communities in the Lincolnshire Wolds were changing.

As the shop became busier with customers coming in for their papers and shopping, we recruited various helpers. Sue Crawford was our first helper, coming in after school on Fridays. When she got married she lived in the bungalow across the road and just as she and her husband were due to return from honeymoon, we got a pram and put it on her roof!

Mr and Mrs Lee also lived across the road. They had owned the shop before the Richardsons. Mrs Lee always kept an eye on things and if she saw strange people about she would ring me to check everything was alright.

Nowadays I have the help of Lynne Parkinson. She comes in one morning a week, and this is my time off. Should I need more time for something, either David or Jackie will come to help.

Rebecca, David's daughter, loves to come to Granny's shop to help and also helps out in her Dad's shop at East Barkwith. Jake also serves in the shop. When he was under-age he shouted for Granny if anyone wanted cigarettes or alcohol.

Customers like to chat to the younger generation. They like to listen to their tales.

I have always said the shop must stay open for my funeral. When Eric died of cancer in 2006, the shop stayed open and I thank the kind lady who looked

Remembrance Day display of poppies in the shop window.

after it that day. We planted a tree in the churchyard for Eric, with a plaque which said, *'Shopkeeper and Woodman'*.

I like to do flower arrangements. I do Christmas ones to sell. For William and Kate's wedding I put my wedding dress in the shop window, along with some flower arrangements. The display was much admired by customers.

For the Diamond Jubilee and Olympics in 2012, I did both windows in red-white-and-blue. An old friend, Eileen, helped me. She has been an important support in my life.

During November the windows are filled with poppies. These remind me of Eric, as he died on November 12, 2006.

Every year, after Christmas, I do the stock-taking. When it's all finished, I paint all the shelves. And in my mind I *must* have it done by January 13, the anniversary of our coming to the shop.

We have had our dramas and excitements over the years, and there have been occasions when we have provoked media interest.

In February 2007 we had an earthquake. Fortunately nothing was broken, although some things did fall off the shelves.

On Friday, December 22, 2011, the bungalow opposite the shop caught fire. Two fire engines tackled the blaze. The smell was terrible outside, but not so bad inside.

Jackie, Matthew and the boys were on an aeroplane coming back from holiday in Egypt. They came so see the happenings on the security camera next day.

In January 2013 we were on the Radio Lincolnshire 'Pirate Gold' programme, as it was our 40th anniversary at the shop, and in February Amanda White

BBC's Amanda White interviews me for Radio Lincolnshire's 'Pirate Gold' programme.

came and interviewed us for BBC 'Look North'.

Prince George was born in July 2013. I did the window out in blue-and-white flowers and borrowed a baby doll from a little girl in the village to finish it off.

In October that year, a BBC crew from the 'One Show' came to film us; David Jason of the comedy 'Open All Hours' was going to be in the studio, and they wanted to show a clip of a real-life open-all-hours shop.

In October 2015 I got a letter from the Queen

thanking me for the pictures I'd sent of the shop window. Matthew made new shed doors but had to cut a hole in one of them for the swallows to get in.

In April 2016, I did a special shop window for the Queen's 90th birthday.

I started serving tea and coffee outside to cyclists and Viking Way walkers in 2016. I painted a bicycle bright yellow and stood a mannequin next to it, dressed in lycra, to draw attention to this new service at the village shop.

I called her 'Eve', and it was amazing how many people did a double-take when they saw her. I also

'Eve' was the cause of many a double-take.

Cyclists and walkers visit the Donington on Bain in droves; many head for the shop, for refreshment.

planted-up two old wheelbarrows.

In November, Jackie took me to Leeds to see the Emmerdale studios. It was a lovely day out, but very, very cold.

Her husband, Matthew, made new external doors for the shed; the others were getting very old.

Also that month, we collected £100 in the shop for Children in Need and a rickshaw with Matt Baker from the 'One Show' came through the village. Lots of people lined the village street including the local school children.

After 40 years of snooker on the full-size table in our snooker shed, we sold the table.

Over the years many men and boys had played in the evenings, but now the players practiced less and, tended to come only on match nights. So the table had to go. Another sign of changing times.

Before taking over the shop, we lived at Poplar Farm, Goulceby, and from our window we could see the Red Hill nature reserve, which is managed by Lincolnshire Wildlife Trust.

For those who don't know (but most local people do), Red Hill is an area of steep grassland and scrub, and includes a disused quarry with exposed red chalk, which gives the site its name.

Despite seeing it every day when we lived at Goulceby, it wasn't until 2017 that I visited it for the first time, to watch the Good Friday service they hold there!

In May 2017, we put a new door on our store room, as son-in-law Matthew had put in for planning permission to knock down all our old buildings, and we needed to be secure.

Two months later we started to empty the buildings, prior to demolishing them. Then in September,

Matthew and my grandsons Jake and Luke started to build the MXR motocross shop and workshop.

I dislike not being in the shop, but I needed a holiday, and hadn't had one for seven years, so my daughter-in-law Sally and her three children stayed and ran the shop, so that I could get away.

My best friend Eileen and I went to Bridlington. Eric and I used to go there for weekends and we went there for our silver wedding anniversary.

We decided to look at Bempton Cliffs. The bus dropped us off at the nearest point but it was still over a mile to walk before we got there. We hardly had time see anything before we had to walk the mile back to catch the bus. David had driven us up to Bridlington and Matthew fetched us home. We had a lovely time.

In December 2015, new people, Adam and Victoria, came to the Black Horse inn, next door. Friday night is fish-and-chip night at the Black Horse and Victoria is kind enough to bring mine round for me.

Many years ago, when Mary Leake was at the village pub, she raised money through the year to give the old people coal and food parcels. I made them up

My son-in-law Matthew and my grandsons Jake and Luke built the MXR motocross shop and workshop next to the shop.

with tea, sugar, butter, soup, a small Christmas pudding, rice pudding, biscuits and lots more.

For World Book Day, 2017, I put a 1906 copy of *Mrs Beeton's Everyday Cook Book* in the window. And I had a very exciting day out with daughter Jackie. We went to the Crucible in Sheffield to watch the snooker (my Christmas present).

We saw Barry Hawkins play, and got Ken Doherty's and John Parrott's autographs on a snooker ball I had taken with me.

In July I went to Walesby Church for the 10.30am service. It was exactly the same time as when Eric and

I got married there. David looked after the shop.

We had a lot of snow in February 2018. It was very windy and the roads were nearly blocked with big, big drifts.

I rang Radio Lincolnshire to see if anyone could bring supplies to the shop. Radio Lincolnshire arrived in a 4x4. They had been to Tesco and bought bread and milk, bacon, cheese, biscuits, baked beans, and lots more.

Jackie put a piece on Facebook and it didn't take long for everything to go. Radio Lincolnshire didn't charge us for the supplies, so we asked our customers for donations to Children in Need.

'Look North' arrived and filmed Jackie and me in the shop with all the snow outside. By Saturday morning all the snow had gone and the roads were clear again.

In 2018 my son-in-law Matthew started taking down the sheds to make way for a workshop, shop and office for his MXR business. It was sad to see Eric's old tools and the sheds he had built demolished, but it has tidied up the yard and I still have my flower beds.

I gave up my vegetable garden and we pulled up

the big hedge that was here when we came. We put in a new fence and it's made it much easier to cut the lawns. The only flower borders are near the house.

It is lovely to have them working next door. If I need help (card machine or the till not working, for instance) I just ring them and Jake pops in.

I had to buy a card machine to use in the shop. People were carrying less cash and we had to move with the times. It works fine until the telephone landline goes down.

We made a new garden for me by the back door and a new gravel area at the side of the old wall. I planted it all up with a passion flower and a yellow climbing rose that would be in flower for June 11, which would have been our golden wedding anniversary. I also planted honeysuckle and wisteria, and Luke kindly put wire all across and up the wall for the various plants to climb up.

On May 3, Uncle Frank died. He had taken me to church when we got married and came and drove the van when we went on holiday.

Jake's dog Bella had eight puppies on May 31. It was a very busy day at MXR but they all went home to see the pups being born.

Eric built garden furniture for sale at the shop. It was very popular.

On October 16, my best friend Eileen died from 'mad cow disease' (bovine spongiform encephalopathy, or BSE for short). Eileen had helped us get the shop and she wrote many of the notes for this story of our lives. Now I have to write them myself. Oh dear—not so good. She's left a big gap in my life.

Another really good friend, Sandra Chambers, died on March 22, 2019. She would occasionally come in for a cup of tea, and we would put the world to rights.

She came on my 60th birthday and stayed from 10am to 2.30pm. We had lots of cups of tea that day.

Some people come in the shop once a week, some come in ten times a day.

If I need help with anything there are lots of people I can call on. When we had all the snow a few years ago, Liam Wallis, from Biscathorpe (about one-and-a-half miles away), helped me get the wholesaler's order in.

All the bread and milk went in one day so I had to have another delivery. They dropped it off at our East Barkwith shop, which is on a main road, and Liam fetched it to Donington for me in his Land-Rover.

My customers are my big family and will always help.

In February, 2019, we had to have our dog 'Spot' put to sleep. The vet came out to us and Jake and I stayed with him whilst it was done. Ivan (who works with Matthew, is his best friend and was his best man) took him to Pawsons in the village, who offer a pet cremation service.

We put some of his ashes with Eric's grave. James went with me and we put some near the big tree in the garden, some in the river Bain and some in Wallis's lake, where we used to take him for a walk.

In the farming community, Pawsons, which is only about half a mile, from us, is best known for its hygienic collection and disposal of farm stock.

When we first came here, they cooked the bones on a Monday. Black smoke poured out of the chimney and if the wind was blowing in the wrong direction you had to keep your doors and windows shut. And you had to be careful about putting the washing out!

The company has been going for over 100 years. Times have changed and these days there's no smell; you wouldn't know what goes on down there.

The only time you catch a slight whiff is when one of the third generation come in for a sandwich on their way to, or from, collecting dead animals. We don't mind, and I don't think they'll mind me mentioning it!

When we first came here, the sheds were open at the front and our little grey mobile shop van fitted in fine. But when we got the big red van *Elizabeth,* we had to adapt the shed.

We put on a tin roof and doors at the front. This made it dry, and a bit bigger. We could restock the van from the shop and keep dry. We could also chop sticks in there.

One day, when the van came back from being serviced at Fenwick's at Louth, I started to restock it, and fell into it! Then I did exactly the same again with the second load of provisions.

I asked Eric what they had done to the van and he said they had put new springs on the van and this had made it a bit higher. Eric had to put a slab of concrete down as an extra step for me. The van was only an inch higher, but it made a big difference.

I must thank Dave Fenwick, now retired, as he sometimes worked day and night to keep the van on the road and ready for the next day. If the van wasn't working I had to ring customers for their orders and then Eric would deliver them in the car. We had to keep the customers happy.

I don't go out much, so Sally, the mobile hairdresser, comes to cut my hair. When we first came here I cut and permed it myself most of the time. I would wash it and put rollers in and then put a scarf on and serve in the shop until I had time to sit under the hair dryer.

Twenty-four years ago, my daughter and daughter-in-law both asked why I didn't just blow dry it. That's when I decided to let the mobile hairdresser come once every six weeks to cut it.

She cuts my hair in the kitchen but as soon as the shop bell goes she has to stop, whilst I go, half cut (if you see what I mean), to serve. I do apologise to customers on hair-cut day.

Any job I cannot do, I ring son-in-law Matthew. When the snow came the other year and the electricity went off, he got the generator going for me. This kept the lights on and the till and scales going.

When we first came, we had a hand till and used weights on the scales. I got the till from Boston and still have it today. It has a handle to make it work. How things have changed.

If I'm out in the street and children see me they always ask why I'm not in the shop, getting their sweets from under the counter.

Son David and grandson James took me to see Jimmy White, the snooker player, in February 2019. We took Eric's snooker cue and Jimmy signed it.

On March 23, 2020, I went to Louth for the last time for a year. The Covid virus had struck and it was the was the start of lockdown.

The Prime Minister, Boris Johnson, made an announcement that schools, pubs, hairdressers and restaurants had to close. Only food shops were allowed stay open. People were put on furlough, with 80 percent of their wages paid by the government.

Next day the shop was open at 6.30am as usual, but it felt weird and frightening, possibly because no-one knew what was going to happen.

This went on for ten weeks and we had to work very hard; Jackie came to help me full-time. People were only allowed to go in their own gardens, and for a walk once a day — or to go food shopping.

We had recently started to sell jigsaws in the shop and these became very popular during lock-down as people sought ways to fill their time. We've sold hundreds since.

Easter was very strange. People were not supposed to go anywhere but it was really hot and they went off to the coast and parks anyway. We bought in extra Easter eggs from our wholesaler, Bookers.

Years ago I would sell over 200 Easter eggs but now I don't sell many, only about 25 in total, but during lockdown, with no-one going to town, I sold about

30 a week for the three weeks leading up to Easter Sunday.

Of course, supermarkets can sell them much cheaper and it's the same with hot-cross buns. When we got them from Curtis of Lincoln, they would come only a month before Easter. Now we are supplied by Starbuck's and, like the supermarkets, they start delivering them just after Christmas!

No racing at Cadwell Park during lockdown, no racing at Market Rasen, no sport, no churches open, no garden centres, and the Humber Bridge stopped charging its toll, so no-one had to handle any money.

Pubs, cafes and fish-and-chip shops were all closed, except for takeaways. Builders' merchants were allowed to stay open. If you wanted the doctor you had to ring, not turn up at the surgery. There were no parties to celebrate VE Day on May 8.

We got 16kg bags of bread- plain- and self-raising-flour, as we couldn't get the usual 3kg bags. We weighed the flour and bagged it ourselves. Even the big supermarkets couldn't get flour.

Tinned stuff soon went too and Bookers didn't send much new stock to start with.

Jackie had put a bit on Facebook to say what we had

on the shelves and people came from miles around. Suddenly folk were home-baking. We got margarine in 2kg boxes and it soon went. Icing and castor sugar were the same, soon all gone.

We could only get baking powder in a big jar, and we would then weigh out smaller amounts, to meet customers' needs.

We got fresh yeast from Curtis of Lincoln, and weighed it out. Customers came long distances to get some as there was no yeast to be found anywhere, except on line. Children were at home at the time, so people were baking their own bread. Cheese and butter went very well too.

We had a two-metre mark in the shop. Customers would come in wearing gloves and face-masks and we had hand-sanitiser on the counter. We also had to keep the counter disinfected. Most people paid by card so they didn't have to handle cash.

Jackie would deliver orders in the village and customers would pay at the end of the week.

The weather stayed warm and dry but nobody could go out unless it was in the garden or for a one-hour walk, run or bike ride, with just their own family.

Our wholesaler, Bookers, said they were stopping

telephone ordering at the beginning of September, so David got me a tablet.

This was a big day for me. Jake had been placing the orders on his mobile phone since the beginning of lockdown and now it was time for me to learn. I thought I'd never be able to do it, but I psyched myself up and after a week I could do it on my own.

Jackie was a great help at this time. I couldn't have managed without her. The shop was very busy; people came to do their main shop as they couldn't get to town.

Children went back to school on September 5, and after that the shop wasn't quite so busy, so I managed to get a bit of rest. The shop opening hours changed. I closed earlier Monday to Friday, at 6pm, and closed at 2pm on Saturday and Sunday. However, I don't like the long nights.

People were still supposed to be wearing facemasks but by now lots were forgetting. The virus was going up again and lots of towns and cities were still in partial lockdown.

We were still busy and still having to weigh out flour, although new stock was coming through better. We could only get frozen peas in big bags, and margarine in big tubs. Some items disappeared altogether and were simply not available.

Christmas was very difficult. The country was in semi-lockdown and people still had to stay at home. The shop was busy and we sold about 25 fruit and vegetable boxes. This had been a year people won't forget.

Eric's mother used to make a chocolate biscuit cake for special occasions, birthdays and the like. Now I make them and an old school-friend of Jackie's, Lynn , still likes me to make one for her. I did send her the recipe so she could make one herself, but it didn't come out right—so one day I'm going to have to show her how to make it.

We had a dog who was always running away so we didn't realise she was in pup until it was too late. She had eight puppies. One day they went to play on my vegetable patch and they trashed it completely. I said they must go.

We're happy to put advertisements on the shop door, so we tried to get rid of them by advertising. It didn't work, no-one wanted them. I rang the kennels at Fotherby and the lady in charge said she would take them. We loaded them in the boot of the car and took them to her. When we arrived she'd changed her mind so we had to bring them back again. We did manage to get rid of them in the end.

We had snow in February 2021 and Jake had just got a 4x4 vehicle. He'd got it to go shooting, but as I had to go to Lincoln hospital for tests on my heart, he took me and fetched me home in it.

Jake's girlfriend, Chloe, tested positive for Covid. This meant closing MXR down and I had to do the shop on my own. David came and delivered the orders.

I was worried I would get it and would have to close the shop, but David did three tests on me. I was clear, and so far have stayed that way. Meanwhile Jackie and family were really not well and I kept taking food down to them, leaving it on the doorstep.

In February, after a gap of nearly five months, I was able to get my hair cut again. Sally, the mobile hairdresser, came from Louth and did a great job.

David took me to the Lincolnshire Showground for my Covid jab. Lincolnshire Showground was one of the big testing sites. He took me again in November for my booster.

Outside the shop on my 70th birthday, with Jackie and David.

On May 16, David took me to Tesco to get my photograph taken for my driving licence because it would be my 70th birthday in July. On the way home we called at Walesby church to put some flowers inside.

It was locked, so I left them outside. I took them to celebrate what would have been our 53rd wedding anniversary.

On July 18, I made lots of sausage rolls, cakes and nibbles for my five grandchildren. They were coming for a buffet that evening to celebrate my 70th.

Coming up to Christmas I made 80 dozen mince pies and 20 dozen almond tarts to sell. Last year I had Chloe to help me, but this year I did them on my own. Jackie and Matthew took me to Horncastle for a meal

—a belated birthday present.

Christmas was a four-day holiday. David shut the East Barkwith shop and Post Office, and the Donington on Bain Post Office in the village closed as well. Not me though. I couldn't close for all that time. My customers come first.

At Christmas, Matthew, Sally and Katie all caught Covid. Fortunately they were not too ill.

I sold lots of logs and coal. It was really cold and we delivered lots of orders to people who were isolating.

About 40 years ago we had a visitor for the win-

Coming up to Christmas, I make dozens of mince pies and almond tarts to sell in the shop.

ter. An owl came and lived in the sheds. We would get dead chicks from Mr Doughty, the head teacher at the village school, and put them on top of the Esse cooker, which was always on in the kitchen.

When they were warm, we would put one in our hand and go outside calling 'Owly, owly'. The owl would come and take the chick out of our hands.

At about 6am, the bread man would leave the day's bread in a tray in the shed. The owl tried to sit on his head, and frightened him, but he soon got used to it. When we were filling up the van at night the owl would follow us into the shop. Then, one day he had gone. We did miss him.

One of the most important things I have in the shop is my 'Big Red Book'. This is where I record the money people spend through the week, and then settle up at the weekend. I have nearly all the 50 books from over the years.

Peter is one of my first customers each morning. He comes for his Sun newspaper, Mars bar and bottle of Coke. Then he goes to Goulceby to feed the Lincoln Red cattle for his uncles, the Parkinsons.

He will arrive in either the Land-Rover, carrying the meal they grind themselves, or in the JCB with big

Peter, one of my regulars, on his way back with his JCB, after feeding Lincoln Red cattle at Goulceby.

bales of straw in the bucket. He calls again on the way back for bread, cheese and pies for his pack-up for the day. If he's working on the land he will call in at teatime for potatoes and eggs for his tea.

Parkinsons fatten their own Lincoln Red cattle from calves and take some to Grantham to the slaughter house to get them ready for the butchers. They sell some for home-freezing. It's very nice—and you know exactly where it comes from.

One day, on the way back from looking at his Lincoln Red beast, Graham Parkinson saw two ambulances parked outside the shop.

Concerned that I might have a problem he stopped and came in. I explained that everything was alright. The crews had been staying at the Black Horse pub next door and were now on their way to Cadwell Park. Thanks Graham.

Over the years I've enjoyed watching nature from my kitchen window while having a cup of tea. I've seen lots of wildlife in the garden and I always feed the birds.

I've seen pheasant and partridge on my vegetable plot and one day, on the gravel out front, I saw a duck with her eight baby ducklings. Unfortunately, they went before I could get a photograph of them.

We had a little white sparrow one year. I think it was an albino.

New Year's Day 2022 was quiet. I opened 8am-12pm and then managed to sit down. Wonder what will happen this year. Covid is now only like a bad cold and people need to isolate for only five days.

In the nearly 50 years we've been in the village there are only three people I can think of who have never moved: Pete Stubbs, Mary and John Sims and me.

Enid Hotchin and the Parkinsons still live in the village but have moved to new houses. Lynne Parkinson moved into a new bungalow and couldn't come to help in the shop for a few weeks. Rebecca came to help instead.

David came to tell me my eldest grand-daughter was having a baby in October. My first great grandchild!

In June, Jake and Chloe went to Grimsby shopping and came home engaged. It would have been our wedding anniversary that day. It's good to have two such pieces of good news.

In July, Curtis, the baker, went into administration. We started to get bread from Starbucks in Market Rasen. It is very good, and cheaper.

August 16 bought rain, rain and more rain—45ml fell between 6pm and 8pm. It very nearly came in the shop. I had to put towels down in case it came under the shop door during the night.

Every time cars and lorries went past the shop a big wave would come up the shop door and try to flood the place. Jake and Luke arrived with a big bag of sand to put in the doorway.

It took me back to when we had the snooker room and rain had got in. We had wet on the snooker table, even though it had a waterproof cover on it, so we had to get a hairdryer on it.

I made a cake for a lady's 100th birthday. Luke likes decorating cakes so he helped me once it was made. Grand-daughter Rebecca makes special cakes to sell in her own business. She graduated from Lincoln University in October 2022.

In June and July, we had a heatwave. Everywhere

When 45ml of rain fell in two hours the street was awash and we needed sandbags to protect the shop from the tidal waves thrown up by passing traffic.

Undeterred by rainy weather, David and his son James cycled over from East Barkwith to see me.

was brown instead of green and Coningsby in Lincolnshire recorded the hottest temperature of 40 degrees. The shop was very hot and I sold a lot of ice-cream and cold drinks.

There's still a shortage of some things from the wholesaler, and because the price of petrol and diesel has gone up to nearly £2 a litre, everything else has gone up too.

Many people are still getting Covid but don't now have to isolate. Some have only mild symptoms but some are still very poorly. The hospitals are getting full again. Lots of customers still do lots of shopping with me, like they did during lockdown when they couldn't go to town.

Shaw's stopped delivering fruit and vegetables. They were worn out. They'd been really busy due to Covid restrictions. We now get fruit and veg from EED and Son, in Market Rasen.

I have a nice sun-trap now where the big lean-to store used to be. It's a nice place to sit and wait for customers because I can hear the shop bell go. Matthew made me a seat from a tree Eric had grown from seed. It had to come down when MXR was built. Janey, a lady from the village, carved Eric's name on the back of it.

On warm nights we sit outside on Eric's seat and think of him.

One Sunday, I went with David, Sally and James for a meal. We had a good ride back through Swallow, Stainton-le-Vale and Thoresway. This was were I was taken as a little girl.

My health has improved this year. The tests I had at Lincoln showed blood pressure problems, rather than heart issues. I still have the same leaky heart valve I had years ago. I've got new tablets for my asthma and I don't need to use my puffer.

At 12.30pm on September 8 came the news that the Queen was very ill and the family had been sent for. She had been on holiday at Balmoral and the family flew up there in the afternoon. It was announced on the 6pm news that Her Majesty had died and Prince Charles was now King Charles III and Camilla the Queen Consort.

The next morning I was up early to get the papers and cut photographs out of them to put in the shop window along with some pearls, white gloves, a black handbag and a slice of bread to represent the marmalade sandwich she had shared with Paddington Bear.

I have a red rose that was given to me one Valentine's Day when Eric and I were on holiday in Bridlington. All the ladies in the hotel were given one and I've kept mine ever since. I put it on Eric's grave on what would have been his 70th birthday, and it seemed right, now, to put in the window for the Queen.

On Sunday there was a special church service in Donington on Bain church. Jake asked if I wanted to go as he would look after the shop for me. I decided not to go, but to watch the coffin go from Balmoral to Edinburgh.

In any case, Uncle Frank's daughter Jane and her husband Simon were coming to see me, so it really wasn't possible for me to go to church.

I was also busy making sausage rolls and scones. I took some to Jean across the road as she's not well, and Digby and Ann (who have edited, designed and published this book for me) arrived just as they were coming out of the oven, so they got some too.

The day before the Queen's funeral a lady called to collect her order. She has done this ever since Covid. She parked up the road as there were two ladies and a man, all in black, standing in front of the shop window display I had done in memory of the Queen.

I had made a white wreath and put it on a plinth in the front of the window.

The customer was very concerned, thinking there must be a funeral in the village. No—the people in

With my grandchildren on my 70th birthday, from left, at the back: Jake, Kate, me, Rebecca; at the front: Luke and James.

black were waiting for a taxi to take them to a wedding.

Another local is Dave. He used to have a stall in London selling ladies clothes and when he retired seven years ago he moved into the village. Every day he goes for a walk one way through the village in the morning and the other way in the afternoon, feeding the horse in the field with carrots.

He keeps an eagle eye out for anything different or unusual and lets me know. He came in to tell me he'd seen a large red wheel and tyre. It's was actually a template for a steam engine that Matthew had bought at an auto jumble at Newark.

When Matthew was there last year, he bought the 'Village Shop' sign which is now on the side of the shop. It only cost him £20 and it looks like new.

Another local is Nigel Smith, whose father worked on the Stenigot Estate 50 years ago. He would call at the shop on his way home on his bike, to buy his baccy. Nigel has followed in his footsteps by also working on the estate and he too would call on his way home on his bike, but to buy toffees rather than baccy, also some of his weekly shopping.

Now retired, he now lives in one of the bungalows

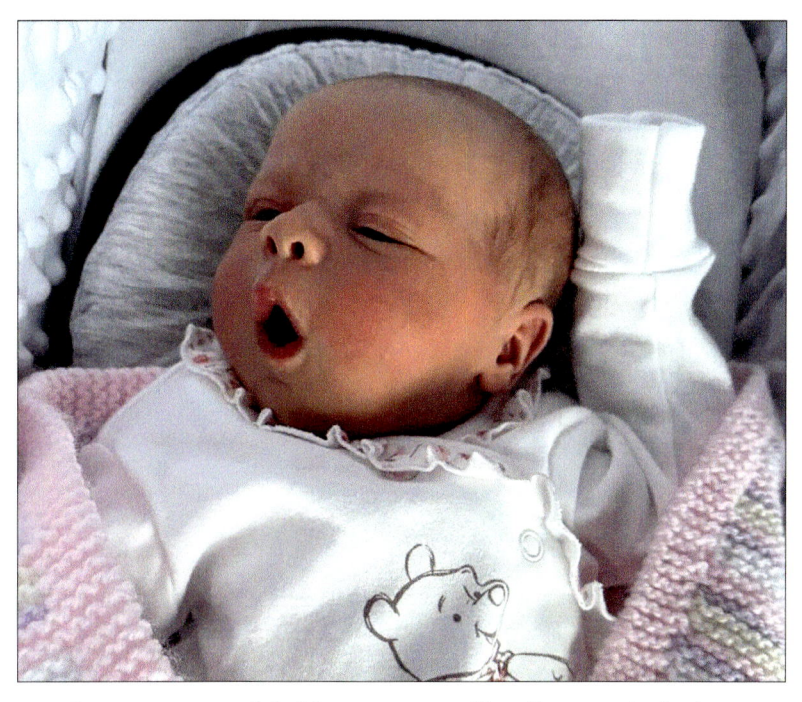

My first great-grandchild, Ivy Rose Hill, 8lb 3oz. It's the beginning of the next generation for the Ward family!

that George Tucker built, and George was another (much loved) local.

One day a lady came into the shop asking for some bananas. I said, 'Sorry, the only ones I had I've just put in the bin'.

She asked me to retrieve them for her and I did. She got them for free, of course. As I said earlier, I can supply my customers with most things!

All my customers are my friends. It's been a privilege to be able to listen to them and talk to them all. Thank you.

My story ends with the birth just hours ago, as I write, of my first great-grandchild. David's daughter, Katie, and her partner, Oscar, have just had a baby daughter, Ivy Rose Hill. She weighed in at 8lb 3oz. It's the beginning of the next generation for the Ward family!

PART THREE: DAVID'S STORY

Why postmasters like me are becoming an extinct species

By David Ward

One of my first memories is when I was around five years old and helped paint our second shop, in East Barkwith—the shop I would end up running, as village postmaster.

When I was six, I walked to the Donington on Bain primary school on my own. We had rather more freedom then, unlike today's children, who are usually accompanied by a parent.

When I was eight, I was sent to Sunday School at the old chapel, opposite the village hall. Sunday School trips to see films such as *Pete's Dragon* at the Kinema in the Woods, at Woodhall Spa, gave me an enduring love of films.

My Father used to tell the story about the time we were in our big red mobile shop making deliveries in the snow. He always carried a shovel so he could dig himself out of trouble if he got stuck in the snow.

Round a corner we slid, and there was nowhere to go but straight into one of our customer's cars. Nobody was hurt, but as I was only eight or nine years old, and watched so many movies, I was con-

One of my evening jobs as a ten-year-old was to fill two-gallon containers with paraffin and load them onto the mobile shop.

The Lyons delivery van called once a week. Note the new bubblegum machine on the shop wall.

vinced the van would explode—so I burst out of the back door in panic, to escape the inevitable devastation.

Nothing happened, of course.

By the time I was ten, every night I had to get all the empty one- and two-gallon containers and fill them with paraffin, then load them back onto the mobile shop. I also had to swap all the 15kg gas bottles for full ones.

I also remember the exciting arrival of a bubblegum-and-tattoo vending machine for the shop wall. The village children would come into shop to swap their 10p coins for five 2p coins to use in the machine.

Then there was the day I had to go with my father

I learned to use the woodyard chainsaws, tractors and Land-Rovers from around 14 years of age.

on the van round and he reversed out and over his dog 'Rex', or it could have been his Dad's dog. Anyway he just scooped the dead dog up and hurriedly buried it in the vegetable patch. Then he carried on with his rounds.

I was always allowed to have the last day of term off school as long as I went on the van round.

Occasionally my father would pull out his binoculars and start checking out the pigeon flight paths ready for a Saturday afternoon off, to go pigeon shooting.

Then he would shower and change for an evening

in our snooker shed, playing snooker with his mates.

My father used his Stihl chainsaw to cut firewood to keep us warm on cold winter nights. Then the logging, or 'wooding' as we called it, took over, and became a full-time business. Eventually we employed four or five people in our woodyard in the village.

Over the years, over 20 people have worked in our business, including my father, mother and sister, his Mum and Dad, Susan in Mum's shop, Gillian in the East Barkwith shop, and of course myself and my wife, and occasionally her sister.

Working in Father's woodyard as a youngster was proper graft.

One day, in the mid-80s, I asked Father if I could put three or four VHS videos on the shelf to rent out to customers. As soon as he agreed, I would scout round all the local shops searching for more tapes to add. Eventually our collection expanded to over 500 tapes, which in due course were replaced by DVDs and Blu-rays.

Around the same time I started cutting the village play area, cemetery and churchyard.

So I would go to school five days a week, then Saturdays and Sundays (after my Sunday paper round) I'd go wooding. Then, when I'd finished wooding for

Sally and I have two daughters, Kate and Rebecca (pictured above in 2012), and a son, James.

Me, with the kids, in one of Grandad's Land-Rovers.

nine or ten hours, I would spend two hours on the ride-on lawnmower.

Eventually, at 15, I decided to go on a business and retail management course at King Edward VI Grammar School in Louth. We had to take two or three other subjects as well, so I chose maths, computer studies and physics.

With hindsight, I wish I'd gone there earlier as the pupils seemed like they really wanted to learn, more so than when I was at Cordeaux High School in Louth.

We had our own business, running the school tuck-shop, making cakes and selling them to the other pupils. By coincidence my middle child now runs a

Sally and me on our wedding day.

successful cake business, called 'Becca's Bakes'.

During my short time at King Edward we had trips to Grimsby to use their retail training facilities and I had work experience, one day a week, in the Wilkinson's store in Louth.

This didn't last long as, to be honest, I already knew a lot of what they were teaching us, as my family were in the business.

I found out I could work for my family's retail empire (three shops, if you include the van) on a Youth Training Scheme.

This worked well because I did all the paperwork. I actually think my parents never touched any of the paperwork; they left it all to me. I filled in all the relevant forms on behalf of my father and the Government paid me £17 a week and—would you believe?—a mileage allowance to drive myself (I was now 17) to our East Barkwith shop and Post Office, five miles away. I remember it was a two-year plan. In the second year the allowance went from £17 a week to £22.50.

I'm sure I would fill in the paperwork stating I was driving from one shop to the other seven days a week, when in reality I probably only worked in the East Barkwith shop two or three days a week, along with two or three days a week on the van round and a day or two 'wooding', which was always proper graft.

I had been learning to use the chainsaws and drive tractors and Land-Rovers from around 14 years of age.

Eventually I was on the Post Office counter in our East Barkwith shop. There was none of this computer stuff then. When I started in 1984-85 it was strictly paper-only.

Then the 'Horizon' computer system arrived. The less said about that the better. Read Nick Wallis's book, *The Great Post Office Scandal,* and I guarantee it will make you weep.

The Post Office and shop at East Barkwith has been in our family for nearly 47 years and I have virtually run the Post Office counter myself for over 30 years.

I've been an active member of the National Federation of Subpostmasters for most of those 30 years, taking on the role of president of the Lincoln and Grimsby branch around five years ago. And this year I became president of the north-east region.

Since the scandalous sell-off of Royal Mail from the Post Office (for which postmasters received nothing, not so much as a 'Thank-you' for the value we added to the sale), it's been a real struggle for postmasters to viably operate their Post Offices. Many, I'm sure, thought they were investing their life's work in the Post Office. We know better now.

Fortunately the Horizon computer nightmare didn't directly cost me or my family anything. But it's been a stressful number of years for us all.

How the Donington on Bain shop used to look before the MXR shop and workshop were built.

More than 700 people were given criminal convictions when the faulty accounting software made it look as though money was missing from their tills.

It's been described as the most widespread miscarriage of justice in United Kingdom history, and dozens of convictions have since been overturned, but too late for some.

It's still costing every postmaster, now and in the future, lost business—lost footfall, and lost commission. I say commission because we postmasters aren't paid a salary. We are self-employed; we don't receive sick pay or holiday pay, or have pension rights. This is

Rebecca helping Granny make biscuit cake.

the next scandal to hit the Post Office.

Royal Mail are stealing our customers and Government are increasingly moving products away from our counters, with some services going on-line, which makes life just that bit more brutish for so many people, especially the elderly.

Meanwhile, we are left offering a free service for the banks.

Banks are closing their high street branches, saving £millions. They no longer have to pay for their buildings and counter staff, or any of the related costs.

We are now performing their day-to-day transactions—cash and cheque deposits, cash withdrawals, balance enquiries and general enquiries. And we do this work for them at a loss, as they don't pay us for the facilities we provide.

The Government, the Post Office and the banks expect us to subsidise the services we offer over our counters. They tell us we should be grateful for the footfall.

Clearly it's wrong to expect our retail business to subsidise the Post Office. It can't carry on, and it won't carry on. So many postmasters are handing their keys back to their landlords, shutting-up shop and quitting, with no pension; in some cases going bankrupt.

In my role as regional president, I've been to London for meetings with Government ministers and charities, including Citizens Advice, to put all these points forward.

These include my personal, some say radical, suggestion that as much as twenty-five percent of the network be paid-off, to make the slimmed-down remainder more profitable.

My other suggestion is a windfall tax on the banks, which are having it easy because we postmasters have facilitated the banks removing themselves from the high street.

It's all very sad. Post Office Limited has just offered an improved pay deal. In some cases it's worth as little as £30 a month extra. That's £30 for 31 days of service. An insult.

As I write, unless this is improved dramatically, thousands of Post Offices will close. In turn all those 'last shops in the village' will disappear.

PART FOUR: JACKIE'S STORY

We worked seven days a week–still do

By Jackie Taylor

When I was 14, I started working at the Black Horse pub in Donington on Bain and carried on there after I left school. I also went tatie-picking and sprout-picking at the Stenigot Estate, just up the road from us. Babysitting was another string to my bow.

At 18, I started work at the Heneage Arms at Hainton (about three miles away), then left and went to college for a year, doing a course in business studies. I got a job at Mayo Workwear in South Yorkshire.

It was whilst working at Hainton pub that I met my husband, Matthew. We were at secondary school together but he never caught my eye. We married on July 24, 1993, and bought a house at Ludford.

We wanted to move back into Donington and Bert Turner approached Matthew and offered to sell us the old school, which had also been a chapel and milking parlour. We bought it, took it down brick by brick, and built our present house.

I worked for Dad driving the mobile shop and serving in the East Barkwith shop. This stopped when I was seven months pregnant and decided to start offering bed-and-breakfast. Two years later we added an extension and the B&B flourished. Jake was born May 25, 2000, and Luke on October 11, the following year.

Dad had the woodyard until he died in November, 2006. In 2018, Matthew took over the yard as a base for his machinery and building materials. Funny how it's all come back to the family again.

Luke works with Matthew on the building side of

Mum and me with 'Elizabeth', our mobile shop. We decided to stop the service in March 2000, when I was seven months pregnant.

the business. He started work as soon as he left school. Jake runs the motocross shop (next to Mum's shop) along with Ivan Kirk.

When the boys were five and six years old, we started motocross racing, travelling all over the country every weekend, either to practice or race. Sometimes they would take a day off school.

It was because of their love of motocross that Matthew started the MXR motocross business. It started off by breaking the boys' old bikes up and selling the

The local Press splashed 'Elizabeth's' retirement.

parts, and from there it just grew... and grew.

Previously, Matthew had been working away a lot, operating heavy plant machines on pipelines, then working for an Astroturf company, building Astroturf pitches at colleges, leisure centres and universities.

Then he set up the MXR business and now also does building and groundwork.

Christmas shows used to be in Mum's front-room and kitchen. I used to sit on the stairs when people came at night to view what was there. It was usually past my bedtime. The show then moved outside to the snooker shed.

When going out with Dad on the van round we would have an early start. We took our lunch of sandwiches and would stop by the roadside to eat them. I can remember they used to be corned beef.

We would get home late, usually after 6 o'clock, and our tea was kept warm in the bottom of the oven. I didn't always like being out on the van but some customers would give me 5p or 20p coins. I put them in my money box.

On Mondays we went to Louth in the van and would park illegally outside the old Curry's shop, waiting for the bank to open, so Dad could deposit the week's takings. We were always early.

From there we went to the Macdonald's bakery on the outskirts of town. We would pick up sausage rolls and pies and have a hot chocolate, then onto a bakery in Aswell Street (where Oliver's Wine Bar is now) to collect trays of cakes. I can still smell them now. Then we came back home, to bag everything up ready for the next day's round.

The van was a game old thing. It used to plough through snow.

On Tuesday's we always had lunch at Granny and

Grandad Ward's at the shop at East Barkwith, and would stay for an hour.

David used to go out with Dad a lot on the van as well as me.

When Dad went into the logging business, he would take the car and trailer to Girsby Woods. We had to barrow the logs through the woods then chuck them over the fence into the trailer.

There were always cows in the field, which meant there were always flies too. Some logs never made it into the trailer. If they landed in a cow pat when thrown over the fence, they stayed there. I was petrified of the cows milling around the car and trailer. However, I did get £1 per trailer load.

I had two Sunday paper rounds. Nearly every house in the village had a paper delivered. I never minded delivering the papers because at Christmas we got presents, or cards with some money inside.

Mum and Dad were always working but in the summer holidays, Mum would take us on a day trip to the seaside. We also went to stay at Granny and Grandad's in the holidays, and this was a treat. We played

Jake and Luke caught crayfish at Biscathorpe (one of our local chalk stream beauty spots) ... and sold them all.

out with friends in the village on our bikes.

I used to bike to East Barkwith on either a Tuesday or Thursday and then get a lift home with Dad in the van. I think I only ever rode my bike once or twice without having to get off it to push it up a hill.

The hunt used to meet at the pub next door when Mary Leake had it. The car park entrance was at the side of the shop (the pub's restaurant room is there

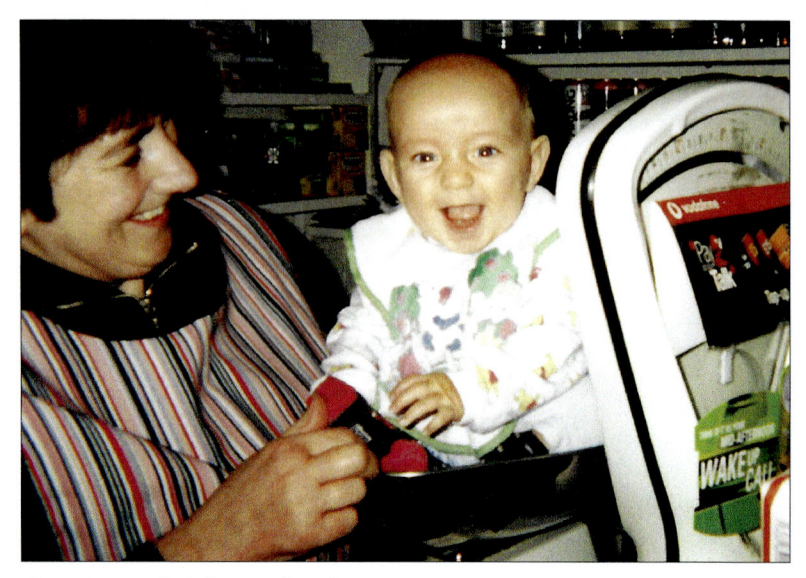

Granny with Jake in the shop.

now).

One night in winter a man collapsed at the side of the house where our drive is. He was rolling around, half on the road and half on the drive. Mum was fretting, as Dad would soon be home with the van and she thought he might run him over—he didn't.

Another time, a car came out of the pub entrance and ran into our front-room door, sending a glass cabinet crashing to the floor and breaking a lot of stuff.

Mum was crying, and I remember ringing the police whilst someone calmed her down. The car drove off. I think the police caught them and found they were drunk.

Our treat on a Sunday was to have either a chocolate bar or an ice cream from the shop.

One morning Dad backed the van out to go on his rounds and our dog Rex didn't move. He ran over him and we buried him in the garden.

I couldn't do head-over-heals so Dad learnt me to do them and made his nose bleed.

One Sunday morning Mum was gardening and

Matthew straps up the wood-saw that claimed Dad's thumb -end, see Part Two (Mum's part), as we prepared to build the MXR showroom and shop.

came in bleeding from her shoulder. She sat on a stool in the kitchen. Fortunately the milkman was there delivering milk. As he came into the kitchen Mum passed out and he caught her.

The Bellamy's lorry used to deliver crates of glass bottles of pop and David and I would get a bottle free for helping. This was a real highlight for us.

Hildred's lorry used to come delivering boxes of chocolates and we used to help the lady (Janet) carry them into the storeroom for Mum to put on the shelves. That same lady had a lorry with an organ on it and she would come to the Bain Valley Hay Days to play music.

Dad would take the van to cricket matches, which were held in a field up Manor Hill. He sold sweets, ice-cream and drinks. Once he took it to Middle Rasen when they had a fete, and again sold confectionary.

It used to snow every winter and Mr Tucker would dig the village out with his digger. On Saturday morning he and Mrs Tucker would come into the shop and buy me a packet of Polos. A real treat.

One year Dad and Phil Crowley walked to East

Barkwith. They just wanted to do something, as we were snowed in.

The electric used to go off a lot. We had a gas-light in the shop for when this happened. In the mornings, I used to scrape ice from the window to see what it was like outside, then get dressed under the bed clothes, as it was freezing. The school was always kept open. It never closed.

Dad used to make (weird) stuff in the garage and we were told not to look out of the window when he was welding.

We adopted a cat. It was very timid and we called it Sisu. Dad got him tamed in the end. He would sit on the flat roof near the chimney stack to keep warm at night.

We used to have a lot of power-cuts, hence the gas-light, ready and waiting, in the shop.

When Dad came in at night from his van round we had to open the gate for him and 'Owly' would fly out of the shed and try to bite us. It was dark and I was frightened every time.

One day our two dogs, Port and Shandy, ran away. They still hadn't returned when I came home from school and I was really upset. Fortunately, someone rang from Hylands Farm at South Willingham to say they were there. I was really happy to see them home again.

Dad used to go shooting quite often and at one time he started to train one of our dogs to fetch the birds back. He shouted at the dog quite a lot. I got quite upset.

I went with him to the pea fields and we set up a hide. I used to go out of the hide and get some peas and would then sit and shell them. When I took them home Mum would blanch and freeze them.

One particular Sunday (it must have been a Sunday as the shop was closed for half a day), Dad went shooting with Mr Whilby. Mum was so cross and upset that she took David and me swimming. That was a treat as we hardly ever had days out, because Mum and Dad were always working.

My wedding day, July 1993.

I can't really remember the holidays we went on or where we went as we were very young, but I do remember being in a hotel and David was sick on his teddy bear. They washed it for him and hung it on the line to dry.

We didn't do shopping trips either. Mum used to make my skirts. I had two white ones with flowers on.

We used to play out on Meadow Croft on our push bikes. I remember coming off mine and grazing my knees. I would then push my bike home and have to have a bath to try and get all the dirt and grit out of my knees.

I was out in the village one day when a car came past with David inside. He was bleeding all down his face. He had fallen off his bike on South Willingham hill on his way to Granny and Grandad's at East Barkwith. I was told to go out and play again while they cleaned him up.

Life has never been boring in our family!